The Life
on Water
AND
THE LIFE BENEATH

J. S. Harry's first book of poetry, *the deer under the skin* (1971), was awarded the Harri Jones Memorial Prize and chosen as the Poetry Society Book of the Year. It was followed by *Hold, for a Little While, and Turn Gently* (1979), and *A Dandelion for Van Gogh* (1985), which was shortlisted for the National Book Council Awards and the Adelaide Festival Poetry Awards.

J. S. Harry has been writer-in-residence at the Australian National University and guest editor for ABC Radio National's poetry programme. A selection of work has been translated and published in Italian, and the title poem from *The Life on Water and the Life Beneath* won the PEN International Lyne Phillips Poetry Prize in 1987.

The Life
on Water
AND
THE LIFE BENEATH

J. S. Harry

Published in association with Paperbark Press

An imprint of HarperCollins*Publishers*

This project has been assisted by
the Commonwealth Government
through the Australia Council,
its art funding and advisory body.

Angus&Robertson
An imprint of HarperCollins*Publishers*, Australia

First published in Australia in 1995

Copyright © J. S. Harry 1995

This book is copyright.
Apart from any fair dealing for the purposes of private study, research,
criticism or review, as permitted under the Copyright Act, no part may
be reproduced by any process without written permission.
Inquiries should be addressed to the publishers.

HarperCollins*Publishers*
25 Ryde Road, Pymble, Sydney, NSW 2073, Australia
31 View Road, Glenfield, Auckland 10, New Zealand
77–85 Fulham Palace Road, London W6 8JB, United Kingdom
Hazelton Lanes, 55 Avenue Road, Suite 2900, Toronto, Ontario M5R 3L2
and 1995 Markham Road, Scarborough, Ontario M1B 5M8, Canada
10 East 53rd Street, New York NY 10032, USA

National Library of Australia Cataloguing-in-Publication data:

Harry, J. S.
   The life on water and the life beneath.

   ISBN 0 207 18453 4
   I. Title.
A821.3

Cover design by Penny Maxwell featuring an original photograph from
Australian Picture Library Pty Ltd

9 8 7 6 5 4 3 2 1
95 96 97 98 99

For my mother, and for Sarah, Andrew, Sally, and Bill

∼

Contents

Acknowledgements *ix*

The Life on Water and the Life Beneath *1*

Peter Henry Lepus *17*

Biographical Notes on the Original Peter Henry Lepus *21*

   Lapin on the Loose *25*
   'South' Country — in 'Value-Judgement' Land — *29*
   An Art Historian with a Church for a Burrow *33*
   Antarctica? *37*
   'Calcutta': *41*
   Small and Rural *42*
   Circles *44*
   Ses Arrière-Pensées — A Rueful Survey *46*
   Rot from the Head Down? *49*
   'Japan' *55*

Paisaje con un Pájaro
or Painting in a Wren? *61*

a green evening *63*

Looking for Some Tracks
(instead of making them) *65*

Rear Vision *68*

An Impression of Minimalist Art in the Late Twentieth Century *70*

As if *72*

Best Lies . . . *74*

her letter . . . *79*

Whistling the Fluff *82*

worn money *85*

Riding Circles *87*

subjective around lismore *89*

Slugs Could Ski *91*

now if you could . . . *95*

another 'red' lady *97*

Mother with Broom *98*

Woman as Jug/ Blue Lady Poem *101*

Navigating Around Things *104*

Incomplete Observation of Process *108*

the coffee *112*

They Do Well *114*

metamultiplexities *117*

Emerson as Brahma *118*

Chorus & Protagonists *122*

for all . . . (1987) *124*

From HIV to Full-blown . . . *126*

with the last of the light *127*

Picking the Nits *129*

The National Glue — What Goes Down . . . Must Come Up? *134*

NOTES *141*

ACKNOWLEDGEMENTS

The Life on Water and the Life Beneath was awarded the PEN International (Sydney Centre) Lyne Phillips Poetry Prize in 1987.

Variations of some of the Peter Henry Lepus poems have been published by *Meanjin*, *The Phoenix Review*, *Salt* and *Southerly*.

The ABC radio programme 'A First Hearing' broadcast 'From HIV to Full-blown . . .' and an early version of 'Slugs Could Ski'.

Poems, sometimes in different forms, have been published in the following magazines and anthologies: *The Australian Literary Supplement*, *Australian Writing 1988*, ed. Manfred Jurgensen and Robert Adamson (Outrider), *Australian Writing Now* (Penguin Books), *Australian Poetry 1986*, ed. Vivian Smith (Angus & Robertson), *Australian Poetry 1988*, ed. Vivian Smith (Angus & Robertson), *Fine Line*, *Hermes*, *Island Magazine*, *The Last Poet's Choice*, ed. Philip Roberts (Island Press), *Meanjin*, *New Poetry*, *Overland*, *The Penguin Book of Australian Women Poets*, eds Susan Hampton and Kate Llewellyn, *The Phoenix Review*, *Poems from the Australian's Twentieth Anniversary Competition*, eds Andrew Taylor and Judith Rodriguez (Angus & Robertson), *Quadrant*, *Salt (The Bird Catcher's Song Anthology)*, *Scripsi*, *Southerly*, *The Temperament of Generations*, eds Jenny Lee and Gerald Murnane (Melbourne University Press), and *Ulitarra*.

The author and publisher gratefully acknowledge permission to reprint the quote from Jacques Lacan, which is taken from *Lacan* by Malcolm Bowie, (published in 1991 by Fontana, an imprint of HarperCollins Publishers Limited). We would also like to thank Basil Blackwell Ltd for permission to quote from Ludwig Wittgenstein's *The Blue and Brown Books*; Viking Penguin Inc. for permission to reproduce, from *The Portable Emerson*, the lines from Emerson's poem 'Brahma'; and the ABC for permission to quote Bob Hudson (from his music programme broadcast by Radio National on 29 June 1991).

The reference dictionaries used have been predominantly those published by Oxford University Press. In particular, the entry concerning 'doily' which appears in the Notes section has been reproduced, by kind permission of Oxford University Press, from *The Oxford English Dictionary*, founded mainly on the materials collected by the Philological Society and edited by James A. H. Murray, Henry Bradley, W. A. Craigie and C. T. Onions (first published in 1933, reprinted 1961, 1970).

Thanks to the Australian National University and to the Literature Board of the Australia Council for a Writer in Residence fellowship, in 1989, which enabled work to be done on the manuscript and some of these poems to be written.

For advice of various kinds at different stages in the preparation of this book, I would like to thank particularly N.S., J.M., D.B., W.G., K.L., D.H., T.C., J.R., J.K., R.H., A.S., and Sarah and Andrew.

Any resemblance to rabbits living or dead is purely coincidental.

∼

The Life on Water and the Life Beneath

No poems can live or please that are written by drinkers of water.

Horace

The Life on Water and the Life Beneath

1

From a book of facts (he was carrying with him): *A man can be said to be insane while still retaining some sanity. There is no omni-valid first point, like a marker of no retreat, beyond which a victim must first pass in order to be seen to be mad. Many acts masquerading as acts of insanity have reasons behind them. Murder is not a proof*
          of madness,
though it may be a sign of it. There is no proved connection between musical creativity and insanity. (or, to put it another way, an indication
that you are not going to be some shit-genius composer doesn't mean that you aren't going to grow up to be a lunatic.)

Ten years since they'd slapped the dam
across the arse-end of the valley.

He was rowing over that lake now, above,
in an imprecise way, the houses
he and others had grown up in.

He thought of the houses as bodies
of human habitation. He wondered
how they were rotting.

Round his neck, as he rowed, over the lake above
the ground he and others had grown both taller and
  broader on,
across new water, Debussy — coming out of the
ear-pieces of the transistor. The
(factual chop, wrapped in a nice paper-doiley)
gentility, of the radio-station's music announcer,
the woody pears, solid green, absolutely juiceless,
of his words' contents,
clashing
against the precise,
otherworldliness of the music:

In this piece, you hear the waves
break, ripple, then build
their tide to crash again
on the spires of the
drowned cathedral.
                    (Clarté! clarté!
Play the piece again, to get it sharper.
Don't leave any of the
spiky — (each stands by itself
but reverberates) notes out of it.)

How to create a music (like it)
                (as original as it was) ever?
Debussy.
Who'd won the *Prix de Rome* at twenty-two.
And went on from it.

2

To remove vagueness is to outline the penumbra of a shadow.
The line is there after we have drawn it and not before.

Wittgenstein

When they'd finished
the dam to drown the valley, it had been summer.
Water gathered slowly, swelling first inside the river.
                 Once
the banks had been breached, there was no point
at which anyone could toss
an apple core and say, *Splash!*
That's the river. From splash-ripples out
the drowned valley starts. A vagueness
grew in people's minds. How could
any memory hold the line
of a water's silver
that had been already thickened
by the expansion of its own colour . . . No one
in his class had drawn it, the river, as it was.
No faithful, following, line of gums
played 'dog' to the river's 'drover'.
Gums
      were about,
                 some near
the river
      some not.

And, grey in winter, green in summer,
tippling constantly,
no convenient
line of drinker-willows
knelt, stumbled, leaned,
stood, or fell,
against their bar
that was the river.

The ford
had a pebble bottom.
Kids plashed there, after small
wet-eyed, leaf-bronze frogs,
as slim as pocket rubbers
and as droppable,
and after stone collections, that slipped
and clinked, against one another
in your pockets.

The water-brilliance of the stones
that you took home
faded into dullness
before you could show a
mother father sister or a
brother.

~

Where is the music for the spread
of water's silence
over landscape. What is the sound
that will silk over your ears' skin
like the silence of water?

~

3

It seemed, to the children watching that summer,
that the water rose almost as slowly, up
from the floor of the valley, as the bald grey hills
above the valley were said by teachers
to be shrinking. If I live ten thousand years
then the erosion of the hills
'll be as plain to me
as a Street's icecream running down in the sun,
he'd once thought, licking one's
rounded top to a point, then watching it deliquesce
as he rode back, one-handed, from the
general store, on his bicycle.
When you poured
water on rock — you got river-sound. When you
rubbed two pieces of rock together to mimic
weathering, the sound was scrape and scratching
like a mechanical rabbit trying to dig up from under dirt.
Where was the music for erosion . . .
The time of the rock experiments was when
water first crept
round the grey, lichened feet
of the river paddock's
hand-axed fence-posts.

Ibis moved in as if to test
the wisdom of the insects
in their new habitat.

Grasshoppers
had water, to gauge, to leap over. If one
missed a tussock-island,
it landed clumsily in water. All legs up and struggling
it was dinner, for a white
or straw-necked ibis.

For months the paddock magpies gurgled
in gums they could not
visit earth beneath, for worms.
Feeding patterns altered.
                    Temporarily
those magpies fed
in space;
        it was miles
to other trees that drew from peckable ground.

School   was moved
from the riverflat to the lower hills
to squat with the hares in the upland grass
above the valley's
final drowning. Easy
to move a one-room demountable.
When the magpies moved
it was their absence
                    rather than
their act of moving out
that was noticed. Absence audible
as a rubber band stretched tight
that your ears
anticipate
the snapping or pinging of.

But the magpies did not
come back
to break the strand of the silence
with their warbles.

~

4

Worms drowned all over the valley
in the silver-clay water, as it rose.
They too rose (pale as the face of Debussy
in the music encyclopaedia)
bloated when their air-holes flooded.

Fence posts
became roosts for waterfowl.
You could travel along
the line of a fence
trailing an oar; there were ants
colonizing the tops
of the fence posts and when
the water swallowed the fences,
where
would the ants go . . .

where was the music for them . . . how
was it . . . how was it . . . to be transcribed?

Swallows pausing briefly
had only the top
rusty strands to sit on
and no answers.

He had seen ants trapped
on an arm of a drowned-man-tree,
its one arm uplifted save me above the flooding,
but caught, bound dead in mediation
between earth, water and air. Islanded.
                    From the boat he'd
watched the ants run, time and time repeated,
to the edge, to the edge of their world,
as if looking for an exit from its ending,
as if in panic; when a leaf-
boat brushed, just once, against the dead-man-tree,
three ants jumped, at that instant, at it, two
fell and were swirled turning
down into the muddy eddies of the drowned things.
                           One
of the three ants made it to the leaf
and was last seen, rushing from one side
of its boat to the other, sailing
as if to discover AntAmerica
already settled, a colony
to join onto? Ready to jump
if a moment of landing
presented itself. Opportunist
as some humans
were not.

~

5

      Ahead, what the ant came to —
was only a beat-up white weatherboard church
that the water sogged into, and ambled around,
inside and out, slowly, unmusically, apathetic
as an end-of-the-day stock horse.
> *If you can't*
> *create an objective correlative, in music,*
> *for your images . . .*

> > *if you haven't enough*
> > *creative imagination in you . . .*
> > *you'd better get out, give up*
> > *your scholarship.*

(All his *études*
were eye-pictures
that his ears
got wrong. His tonal compositions
were banal.)

> The pantomorphic
> nature of water.

> You could count
> the shapes it fell into,
> never the substance.
> Put water in glasses,
> litres, tonnes:
> you count the measures;
> there is always water
> water uncountable
> inside them
> outside them.

                                        He
                                        had made nothing
                                        for water.
                                        Even Pythagoras,
                                        that ancient
                                        picker and piler
                                        of pebbles, that
                                        ingenious mechanic,
                                        discovered, with string
                                        and mathematics,
                                        something durable
                                        for music:

The full string
sounds the tonic.
Clamped at ¾, it sounds
a fourth higher.
This shortened string
is now clamped at
⅔ of its length, sounding
a fifth higher still.
The final length
is half the original
and sounds
an octave above it.

The out-of-tune piano'd
been moved, from the church, on the
back of someone's ute
on the last
Sunday before the
drowning. They'd not
played Debussy on it, found him

somehow wrong . . . as Gilbert and Sullivan . . .
were endlessly right,
for the church music society's
musical socials.

~

6

     La cathédrale engloutie
he had found, had found him, last year
at the Conservatorium.

        Once tears
        have run, down a face,
        they too
        are uncountable.
The waterbirds had screams of murderers
and draggle-dipped their legs
as if to wash
a victim's blood off
as they flew. Uncle James
the local maniac had been discovered
screaming when he'd stepped, protected in the
cloak of his madness, into the iced white
          winter river
to wash the sticky red off feet and axe. His banal — sane —
reaction
to his body's struggling in ice
had uncovered his madness. Victims were close.
Like a grotesque butcher-bird
he'd impaled their shortened forms,
after death,

on stakes he'd sharpened
to receive them.

Was it an 'advantage'
to be related
to an axe murderer; if so
it was one he'd not looked
to uncover.

Uncle James
was a fact
he'd buried almost longer
than he could remember.

Age five, age six, age seven —
somewhere there.

There were no such
marks, going down, into the dammed valley,
to measure its depth.
A year ago when he'd jumped
out of the boat, to imagine better
the spires rising, the sounds
of the bells ringing, underwater, he'd had
to hang, clinging, to the boat's sides,
could not touch bottom.

~

7

Mist
passed overhead and rested
itself on the ground, wandering like a sick animal
getting up, lying down, all night.
                                                          Like a dog
he'd had that was hit by a car, that dropped
and struggled up, all through
the dark, as if it were afraid
if it stayed down
it would be dying.
On one side through the morning's clouds
there was a thin strip of gold light as if
the weather might be clearing. When he got
to the place far out
where the smoky cloud and the light rain
blurred the boundaries,
he was going to take
his transistor off, place it carefully
inside the holey doiley of his sweater
in the bottom of the boat, then
he was going to find the drowned cathedral.

~

When water fills your ears
and you hear nothing
you have a few moments
in which to try
to imagine

~

how to make
the unbearable
sound

Peter Henry Lepus

It is more important that a proposition be interesting than that it be true.

A. N. Whitehead
Adventures of Ideas (1933)

*And sometimes when people went on the roads
they changed their lives.*

Bob Hudson
ABC Radio (29 June 1991)

Biographical Notes on the Original Peter Henry Lepus

Peter Henry Lepus has been named by his mother, an extremely well-read and well-educated rabbit of Creole ancestry, after a character in a book of old Creole folk tales, *L'Histoire de Pierre Henri Lepus*. However he is a British rabbit and his mother has always called him *Peter* Lepus, rather than Pierre, although pronouncing the 'Lepus' with a slight French accent, out of deference to the Creole, so that the final syllable sounds the same as the vowel at the end of the French word *'chou'* and has a pleasant sound when you call it across a grassy meadow in the evening. Sometimes she calls him Peter Henry, or Peter L. Most frequently she simply calls him Peter. He has become accustomed to pricking his ears to all of these names.

He has at times been something of a disappointment to his mother, possibly as he has turned out to have a somewhat different character from the Creole hero after whom he was named.

It is uncertain whether the Creole hero's family name was originally 'Lapsus' and the 'p' became somehow disconnected, losing itself in one of those gaps in time or memory, emerging unpredictably (much later) on the ground of the word's wornaway, first 's', or 'Lapus', which the hero's mother might have thought ugly. It was she who revised it to 'Lepus', the Latin for 'hare', which she probably knew was their species name . . .

Unlike his namesake, Peter Lepus grew up in the English countryside of the early twentieth century, where he was exposed, to a degree, to the culture of that time. He was put into a children's book at an early age and has travelled extensively.

Occasionally finding perplexing drawings of himself torn from the pages of the rare, first English-language-edition of *Peter Henry Lapus* (where the surname is misspelt consistently on both spine and title page) on the walls of the Great Rabbit Burrows of France and Germany, Peter Lepus was also puzzled to find images of his greybrown self nailed to the lower well-nibbled boles of trees in more distant countries. Sometimes these images of himself had small round holes in them. (Some biographers have speculated that Peter Lepus' later interest in philosophy may have stemmed from the sight of such almost-perfect near-circular enclosures. There is ground for disputing this.)

It was not to be predicted that when *The Tale of Peter Henry Lepus* had reached the ears of almost every rabbit household in Britain, it would be re-invented, so it could enter burrows in diverse new places, including, later, Spain, nor that its small rabbit persona should be analysed, for improprieties 'mental and moral'*, in an essay-*cum-laude* by Graham Greene, or psychoanalysed, even though somewhat disrespectfully, by some post-modern students of Freud.

Peter Henry Lepus, the book of the early childhood, became a classic and a standard text for Children's Literature courses. However, as Peter L. never hopped as a student through those particular hedgerows, he

---

* This may be a reference to Peter Lepus' later studies in philosophy, which, according to Rush Rhees, was known at Cambridge as 'Mental and Moral Sciences'.

remained largely ignorant of his 'life' in other people's psyches, and of his 'status' in those remote, perspicaciously observed yet for him somehow 'bladeless' fields.

There is a tale passing as truth in Baton Rouge today, in rap song form, among the musos in some of the smokier bars, that Peter L. met Wittgenstein in Vienna in 1902 and disputed with him on the aerodynamics for an airborne bicycle, with trainer wheels for learner-flyers. In some raps, the bike is a winged, prototype-jet (two-wheeler), with optional extra ailerons for would-be *high*-flyers. This fine flying 'history', the details of which the singers vary endlessly, apparently unconsciously, steers away from biographers' facts and dates, at almost all its points. (Perhaps the tale and its tellers share, with the hare family, a rabbity habit of wiping one's chin in scorn on those combinations of things — or states of affairs — for which, for whatever reason, one has contempt? Including death?)

In 1902 the young Wittgenstein was being educated at home. He was thirteen and had thought about suicide. He had not yet begun to study engineering. His knowledge of the mechanics of the wheel was slim. All he had managed to design, even by rumour, was a slightly working copy of a sewing machine. His interest in aerodynamics surfaced only in 1907, after he had spent three (miserable) years at school and a further three (unhappy) terms at Tech. He did not attempt to acquire the maths for aeronautical design before 1908.

Peter L. had, up to 1902, no awareness of aeronautics and little knowledge of mechanical engineering. His only experience with wheels had been with the sort that were attached to the open, horse-drawn village carts, carrying away those disagreeable humans he hoped the weather would deeply discomfort by dousing them with buckets of icy sky-water.

Early family portraits, dated 1902 in brown ink on the back, show a young and tense Peter Lepus, scenting danger, peering stiffly out at the third year of the twentieth century, from behind the ampler bodies of the older aproned rabbits in his family, as if he feels he needs their bulk and kick-power to protect him. (But from whom? And why?)

He appears far too small, in the year of the brown-ink portraits, to have been able to travel to London, stow away on a ship, or reach Vienna by himself.

Around about the time A. N. Whitehead and Bertrand Russell were working their way towards *Principia Mathematica* (and perhaps before Wittgenstein had arrived in England, to 'discover' and become, briefly, a student of Bertrand Russell), Peter Henry Lepus was provoked into trying to use his mind . . .

It is perhaps from this period onward that his sense of deracination and disorientation becomes more pronounced . . .

Peter Henry Lepus

Lapin on the Loose

1 'UNDER DROUGHT'

    Like a pirated edition
of the book of himself
    the eponymous Peter Henry Lepus
gets dumped in Australia.

Forty per cent of it
    is 'under drought'. Peter Henry
has never been 'under drought' before —
    only under fences & gates.
He wonders if it is anything like
being 'under the doctor', as a man he met
    by the railroad track told Peter
the man's missus was. The Australia
Peter is in looks very large & brown.
    Rock-piled hills wear hats of shade
where rabbits are lying around.
    Somnolent rabbits with sick red eyes
stir sluggishly to glare at him — an interloper,
    in exile. *We are replicas of the spirits*
of rabbits who have died
    by mosquito-bite disease,
they inform.   He
has never heard of mosquitoes — or bite-disease —
& doesn't much care why
    strange rabbits died.

Lean, listless, cotton-coloured animals,
    with their fur hanging down
in draggly oily curls — as if their mothers
hadn't been near them with brushes for centuries —
bleat languidly at him, from a stony,
cotton-coloured ground. Some — the more alert —
    are clustered
round a dry, white-crusted lake.
You can't drink here — it's salt,
they baa importantly at him. They
are waiting for a ship
to go to the Middle East,
but there has been a war on —
    their 'holiday'
has been put off; the sheep-
tour advisers bleat
    it will be months
before their 'cruise''s number
comes up. Peter isn't thirsty. Baas
are a bore. *Where is my mother?* he yells,
from the middle of a sand dune's
slope, standing — to see if he can *see* her
from higher up. This ground is hot.
Then he squats.

    He is bitten, by small black
maddened, running things
    which stink when squashed. Enraged,
more & more of them pour upward
out of a hole. *There are thousands of us
underneath you,* they sign
six-legged at him. *You are sitting*

on our house. He moves out. Fast.
Fast is what he has to do:
there are no grass blades,
cucumber frames or radishes,
out here in the fields of sand
on the Desert of Sense.
Nothing to eat, he moans
as he mouths the roasted sand.
It is so horrid they don't even need
    fences & gates to try
to keep a good rabbit out.

2 A GOOD RABBIT?

He meets a travelling
flock of boastful galahs
who tell him they are poets of the feather.
We are the mistresses & masters
of beauty, they yell. *Come with us*

to the Balmain
Brolga's & we will show you
how to strip
shed leaves &
nest in holes
but Peter doesn't believe
they know what they are screeching of . . .
What is beauty? Is it grass?
They do not ask him
to come to *grass* with them . . . *Where is grass?* . . .
    Weeds would do.

One of the unwell rabbits drags itself past.
Are there any dandelions round here?
Peter asks it politely . . .
> A weed is not a weed
> to a rabbit: it is food . . .

or a place where the baby beans
hang down crisp & low — rattling
the old beans' leaves — for a game in the sunset,
to annoy them —
so a rabbit on its hindlegs
can reach up & snap them off?

But the rabbit is too busy —
it is going down a long dark tunnel inside itself
to a ground
where it has never been before. The eyes
it looks at the world with are losing interest.
It does not answer Peter. Its whiskers quiver.
Peter leans closer to hear. *How beautiful*
grass is . . . it breathes, almost with no air.
Then it gives a long slow exhalation
as its lungs say goodbye to the world.
Peter has never seen a dead rabbit before.
He goes round it on all fours sniffing.
This rabbit looks just like the live ones.
Perhaps it will wake up, presently,
& talk to him.
But the rabbit does not wake up
so, after a little wait, Peter Lepus moves off.

'South' Country — In 'Value-Judgement' Land —

1

Old Mrs Rabbit told him
always to keep
his bump of locality
about him. He was never too sure
what she meant: it seemed to shift around
depending on
where she was. Perhaps *she* kept it hidden
safe — for him —
& it only worked
when *she* sat down?

                     Anyrate, now he seems
to have lost it.
            At the top of a good,
rabbit's back-scratching post, he comes
to a square bit of lettered wood
                           which spells:

YOU ARE STANDING ON 43 BLENDS
OF DUSTED-OFF & SUNDRIED RATIONALISM
WITH SOME GROUND UP & ROASTED THINKING
thrown in — all shaded brown
like Nescafé — or philosophy — with
similarly pleasant
addictive smells: YOU ARE SUPPOSED TO PICK
                WHICH BLEND OF GRITS
                MAKES BEST SENSE
                FOR YOU TO CHEW:

but Peter doesn't read it. To him, the sign
is a bit of wood squiggled on with crow-droppings.
                There was a crow
                perched above, which flapped off
as he approached — as if something
                had frightened it.
                He does sit,
for a little rest, in the patch of shade
the big board makes   for a few rabbit-
                                moments
                                scritch scratch
                                with a paw
                                in the earth which
                                he now
                                finds no longer
                                hard-sandy
                                but damp
                                & darkish
                                cow-dung-brown.
Encouraged, moving steadily at a slow lope as if
he is going to no
particular place, & will take days
to get there, he comes, down tors, & round food-bare
                                            rock ledges,
to the grasses of small settled farms. Comfy pigs. Comfy
   cows.

Value-judgements're swirling like Either/Or birds
each in their subjectivity's singular colours
over one end of a valley, & down to its grainrich, sunlit
   floor.

Over furrows & fissures & flaws in the ground,
a dead man comes walking towards him — telling him
it is the South Country. *It is ugly*, the dead man moans;
Peter Henry Lepus sees it as pretty.

2

                By a barn
a man with a huge shining face like the moon
& no fur on his head

                is washing a pig. Peter Henry
goes closer
to see if it is clement . . . to ask for direction.

He hears the man muttering, half to himself —
& half to the pig — but crossly — over & over —
    HOG WASH! HOG WASH!
His voice — has sticks swishing in it . . .
as if it is knocking nuts off a tree
or slicing the heads off weeds.
                Peter thinks it would be safer
to talk to the pig — so he squeaks — very softly —
as a rabbit kitten would — to it, but the man
hears & answers, with great civility, using some
of the loveliest words
that Peter has ever heard
only he cannot remember them,
that he is cleaning the pig up to enter it
in a poetry show, that, if it is like last year,
ninety-eight point six per cent — of the
poems in the show will be 'hog' — 'washed to death' —
                & the other

one point four per cent — diversely — less 'pure' —
              & he is putting
a real, washed hog in, to show them the difference
a bit of wormy life makes . . . He has the crate ready
to enclose the pig, which he points Peter towards,
inviting him . . . with one enormous paw. *There is room
in it for more* . . .
Peter doesn't want to be washed with water —
de-furred — & scrubbed till his skin squeaks
like the hog. He thinks the show
must be a bad place to play
if all the other pigs
are as clean & un-fun to play with
as this cold, stopped pig —
      it has been washed
         with very chilled water —
standing stiffly
on the pained ground. He hears his mother's voice in
   his ears —
she is coming from long ago & far away — telling him
what his brave uncle heard, when he
went looking for the remains of Peter's father —
in Farmer McGruber's garden:
The only good rabbit is a dead rabbit,
sings Farmer McGruber.

An Art Historian with a Church for a Burrow

Looking for the grass
growing sweetly round the graves
in a forgotten churchyard, in Russia,
in April nineteen ninety one,
Peter comes to a dilapidated
human work of stone — crammed
with disintegrating ancient books,
one-of-a-kind manuscripts,
& crumbling first editions.
A book louse with her
home under the rubble tells him
once there were one million tomes.
A Russian art historian with a nimbus
rises as if hallowed
above one of the fonts. *We must
give them back — to the world* — he thunders
— from somewhere deep inside his rabbitcoat —
with a fine, ancient, Slavic passion.
He is not talking of 'Hitler's' books — which Peter
is peering at — with interest — but of the
million or so paintings & *other* rare
objets d'art, that were 'acquired' — by a strange
troupe of Germans with death
as their end-play
who set up a tyranny — long ago —
to act their death-games out

over as much
as they could manage
of the world.

There is a rat sitting on one of the shelves.
*Who is this . . . Hitler with his name
all over the book-plates?*
he squeaks indignantly. *These tomes
are too old & dusty
to taste good. Some of the paper in them's
over two hundred years old. The dust
makes my wife sneeze. The ink
gives my children indigestion. In the winters
they smell dank & taste of mould. It is not
a ripe & savoury mould
such as one finds
in the best blue cheeses.
These rank & malodorous books
are a most unsalubrious diet
for a family of elegant rats
whose aristocratic ancestors
once owned a dacha.*
     *Had the run of it
for free — more likely*, sniffed a sceptic
        outsider rat
by the door.

  *Thickcrusted hunks
of grainy bread, fruit tarts, great wedges of cake —
& Danish cheeses — I would like for my children —
as once I had*, the rat rants on stubbornly,
though nobody seems to be listening.

Most of the people
these artefacts belonged to
were murdered in the ways of the human race
that are most vile, continues the historian.
The thunder in his voice
has moved a little further out
& is muting itself. A quieter
desperation, instead
behind his tone. *But the owners may have descendants*
or at least . . . countries . . . to which
      we could give these stolen world-works back.
    We too stole them when we entered Berlin
as the booty of a war — & we — it is our duty — should
    give them back . . . though we cannot
raise the dead, to do so — or grant them justice.

Peter's paw goes up to his mouth. His attention
wanders out, beyond the beard & the talk, to a distant,
odd & ill-looking tree.
If 'duty' & 'justice' are foods —
& you are hungry for them —
perhaps you should put them inside you?
Grass . . . belongs to the rabbit that finds it.
Trees . . . stand . . . & anyone with teeth
can chew at them. Any bird
with wings & a warning call
can fly to a branch & sing. Ground
belongs to the paws that pad over it
in the moment of passing.
He is not too sure
who owns the rest . . .
A million things — whether edible

or not — seem too many
for one bearded rabbit to store in its burrow —
or even for a colony with a warren to hold.
Perhaps they could take 'Hitler's' books —
& the paintings & chairs — to some big
Village Bazaar, & sell or swap them,
so the rat & his family —
perhaps . . . his cousins too? — other animals
                                      if there were
                                      any spare? —
could have good food?
Outside this cold, stone burrow,
there is warm, fine,
free sunlight . . . belonging to any
                body that can feel it . . .
to which, gratefully, Peter scampers out.

Antarctica?

On his way — to visit the *Tractatus* —
where he thinks to find a brave bed
of young stouthearted lettuces,
to fill in the depression in his middle
as well as the grave hole in the afternoon —
Peter Henry Lepus gets lost
in Kant's *Critique of Pure Reason* . . .
Pictures . . . of MAN . . . & a MOUNTAIN . . .
& later, men — at least two,
& mountains — ditto two. Chinese Edition.
No alphabet. Scuttering over the pages
he is sure his mother would've found
bright & sane as a well-earthed warren
tunnelled carefully out of fresh, soft,
dangerously tumbling sand, Peter discovers no carrots.
He cannot find a lettuce anywhere.

Wittgenstein
comes walking towards him
down an iceberg. He is followed
by a crowd of students
who levitate — six inches
above the ice & higher
than Wittgenstein, though they seem
less solid. More ethereally dressed.

          Now advancing, now retreating, they
& their garments
                swirl
                        around Wittgenstein,
                                        in an icy,
            avid mist.
Wittgenstein is wearing
                  an anguished
look of concentration — wall-to-wall pain stretched tight
across his face. Uncaught & not yet clear thoughts
are hiding in his pockets — roosting
just out of range — like wily
feral hens. His stretching ice-stiff fingers,
curling towards them, cup them & become warm as eggs.
He is wearing a snowy, papery cloak
with black signs, that Peter
does not know are German words, pinned
sparingly to it. Peter does not read
put-to-gether-German-alphabet, yet.
The signs translate: *Go
back. Carrots are
in the world of empirical facts
& growing in the fields of
the live humans
who plant & work them* . . .

YOU ARE IN THE WRONG PLACE.

Peter reads the snow
with his nose, for tracks of scents.
He cannot smell his mother; his sisters,
Turvy, Bolter, Scuttle-butt, & Somersault,

might as well be dead.
Fact: he cannot smell:
his nose is too cold.
He does four or five small
hard pellets to cover his
embarrassment . . . which is invisible
to anyone except himself — & also
as a kind of shame-faced test —
because a rabbit that can't defecate
leaving visible evidence that another rabbit —
if there were any round — could see —
is likely to have transgressed
into death,

& shuffles about a bit
on the white, slippery world —
upon which, mistakenly,
he thinks to sit.

It occurs to him —
there are no other rabbits round —
to test the test.

As he slides
lugubriously down
the hard
ice of a floe, killer-whales,
with a piteous dinner-longing
on their faces, rise up critically —
lunging — to assess him —
a small —
bite-size —

tear-soggy rabbit, in a blue
snuffle-sodden jacket, not at all
distinguished — here — in his poem of woe.

Ringing in his ears,
as he slides
towards the killer-whales
who're now   halfoutof the water —
in their paroxysm — to get at him —
the one thing
that Wittgenstein said,
that Peter heard . . .

(Not
Do not believe all
of the Tractatus Logico-Philosophicus . . .

It is our language that determines
our view of reality, because we see through it . . .
not vice versa . . .
Go piece-meal, but)
Watch out for the (written)
           intoxication of the mind
& the (spoken)
           intoxication of the jaws.

'Calcutta':

French beans think they are on the wrong land mass
& wither into desiccations of homesickness.
Peter Henry Lepus gets lost in 'Calcutta'
on his way to visit Farmer McGruber's vegetable patch.
It is not clement for lettuces in 'Calcutta'
or carrots either. Unfortunately
it is very inclement there
for the famous fat little British rabbit.
He is pursued by hordes who have
bones poking through the lines of their arms.
Very unfriendly. While running
lappity lappity — rather fast — to get away —
he cannons into the lower portion
of some hard legs hiding under a sari.
When Peter looks up — he sees a warm face
rumpled with brown hillocks & little friendly furrows
like a dug vegetable patch in Farmer McGruber's garden.
Peter *is* pleased to see it — & is 'rescued' —
grabbed by his ears — rather roughly he feels —
by Mother Teresa, who plonks him sternly
into a liquid-textured *lapin* version
of the miracle of the bread & the fishes.
Peter isn't hungry any more — & neither
is 'Calcutta'. No one
has camomile tea, after supper. French beans
have finished withering. They are dead. 'Calcutta'
is doing very nicely & thanks you for asking.

Small & Rural

Peter L. is twisting
                  this way & that
                time-jumping
in & out of the texts he is — here — there —
squatting briefly, to sniff the air above,
both of his ears erect as he listens
to the texts' echoes getting fainter & fainter
. . . like a mother's disappearing coo-ee . . .
Rabbits   can hear a car door slam —
      & a favourite text disappearing —
      even from half a paddock away —
      even in 'x' where the word
      paddock once came from . . .

      a small field or enclosure, usually a plot
      of pastureland, adjoining a stable . . .

                            to which
    place a mother perhaps may have gone? . . .

But the word *paddock* also was used
      to stand for a toad —
      probably from Old Norse *padda* —
      & for a frog.

Peter doesn't have much time
>   for frogs, preferring
>   his own hopping,
>   but paddocks are all right,
>   especially if they have grass in them
& the pads & stink
>   of the dog fox & vixen are absent . . .

~

That A Text Should Incorporate
— or try to — Criticisms Of Itself
is a favoured padmark of all
— & only — the textual foxes.

Circles

When he wakes, Russell is standing over him.
W. & I have argued for three days, he says.
His new work is important, & original —
but I am not at all sure
that it is true. Peter sees the tide has come in —
underneath all the buildings. The shrine
seems to be floating. Russell says it looks
like a mother-duck building, surrounded —
at discrete intervals — by the smaller
wooden ducklings of the lesser shrines.
Peter does not know about that.
He hasn't seen many ducks . . .
                    Once he caught a glimpse
of the Waddle-Splat girls — but they
were upside down in a pond & had
wispy bottoms where their heads should be.
They did, perhaps, look a bit like shrines.
What were their names? Becky . . . Jemmy? . . .
It has got dark. There is no moon.
Wittgenstein has paid for the priests
to light the stone lanterns in the pine trees
& has taken his shoes off. Peter wonders why
because the ground is so cold . . .
Perhaps it is Wittgenstein's bedtime?
W. does not tell him & goes off to look at holes
in the ground in the dark
under trees that are farthest
from the priests' holy glow.

Peter thinks if his mother were out at night,
& so sick she got lost, & their burrow were under
those pines, she would know where to come.
Russell looks out at the lights:
Each one is shut in on itself like a human being
he notes. *None of the light circles touch one another.*
At the edges the light gets gradually darker — ;
it's not clear where light begins & darkness stops.
Wittgenstein will write about this.

Ses Arrière-Pensées —
A Rueful Survey

Standing (he's
plain as a target)

unguardedly squatting
(*with trust!*)
on ground where blackberries
creep with stealth

losing his footing
sliding
down hills of obdurate rock

stopping too long
alone in the open
betrayed by the juice of the clover
& the texts of the spring his mouth
full of grass

what has the rueful
Peter Henry Lepus
to cover his arse?

(More like the stub
of a tale
than A Tale?)

A white fluff powder-puff
— of mingy dimensions — ?

Ephemeral stillness?
A (rabbit's?)
           dodgy
talent for flitting?
(What use *are*:)
Anthropomorphic habits?

What has a fox got
to cover its rear? (In retreat!)
An **ENORM-
ous brush!** The colour
of marmalade if you
made it from ginger.
Lucent . . . with rude foxy health.

Peter L. sits kicking at the texts.
He is cross with them

or rather he is cross with himself;
he is kicking — in this instance —
logic texts because *they*
are so unremittingly exact
& *he*
is so unfailingly *errant* . . . A woman professor
who sat on . . . committees of rabbits for years . . .
told him, right at the beginning . . .
No rabbit's rear
was ever covered by its tail
even in the most

'optimistic'
of the rabbit epics . . .
Saint Rabbit the Dragonslayer . . .
or Crusader Rabbit
set in the eleventh century . . .

Rot from the Head Down?

Later when Peter
tells Russell
how it was — for him —
in Russia — in nineteen ninety one —
Russell says, It was quite different
— in nineteen twenty — when *he* was there;
watch was kept — on visitors — & those they met —
    & people
            'eaves-dropped'
on him & the members of the Labour deputation
                with whom he'd gone
to Russia.
      Peter wonders
what 'eaves-dropping' is . . .
His mother has told him
about eaves that hang
out over the edges
of humans' houses —
but those eaves did not
drop off the houses —
Perhaps houses' *rooves* in Russia
fell off on Russell & his friends
wherever they went? Russell shakes his head.
           More than once.
It grieves him to think of how
life was — in Russia — then — for Russians. His face
is a field of remembering pain . . . Middle of the nights
he could hear the sounds

of imprisoned people — being shot —
for being 'idealists'. People he met
were too afraid . . . of being suspected
of mouthing 'wrong' viewpoints — to try
to hunt — with logic — for any
kind of truth. Everyone was afraid . . .
as the scaredest rabbit . . .
of the fox behind the tallest grass . . .
or lurking . . . outside the burrow . . . of who
might be waiting to grab them — for killing —
when they came out.
The four 'most eminent' poets in Russia
were stick-thin, filthy & dressed in rags
when they came to visit Russell
at his hotel. One of them
was allowed — by the Government —
'to make his living lecturing on rhythmics'
but they kept trying to force him to teach it
from the point of view of Marx. He told Russell
to save his life he couldn't tell
how the views of Marx came into
beat & stress & the fall
of syllables, nor had
he been able to work out
how when the ears
hear rain pelting onto a tin roof
they can be taught to recognise
the plonk of a Marxian raindrop
— as distinct — from any other —
in particular — from a Capitalist raindrop.
Russell couldn't help him.

Someone 'high-up' — in the 'equal' government
    confided
        to Russell, it was felt —

if they could get the near-moribund
necrotic-tissued 'body' of their country working —
    by economic theory —
they could put the 'soul' back in
        later . . .
literature, art, music, et cetera . . .

Russell tells Peter, about this — as a theory —
in nineteen twenty he'd had profoundest doubt . . .

To say "I have pain" is no more a statement about a particular person than moaning is.

Wittgenstein, *The Blue Book*

'Japan'

Enormous legs of raddled wood
stand out in water . . . as if they had
been wading . . . on some invisible path,
got tired . . . & stopped & stiffened there . . .
Maybe they'd been plodding out
towards a pine-furred mountain, that *might*
have good burrow-holes in it? Peter
would like to get to it. The mountain
is getting its paws wet in a huge water
that Peter, on the other shore,
does not know is sea. He is on a rim
that reeks of what is outside his experience.
Polluted fish are starting to be dried —
their little bodies laid out on the rocks
in absolute surrender — as if they are offering
what's left of themselves up
to whatever gods may be. Nearby
old men with bark-wrinkled faces
are moving their fingers in & out of holes . . .
as if they were mending . . . like his mother
used to mend small rabbits' clothes. They seem
to be making the big holes into smaller ones.
Perhaps it is a trap to catch blackbirds
that Peter has seen, once,
flung over parts of a pear tree
near the orchard wall. But where
are blackbirds, pear trees, here?

The shore Peter is on has only small pebbles,
rocks, boats, men — & the strange smells.

Sitting with his head in his hands but still
achingly attached to the rest of him, on one
of the rocks, is Wittgenstein. When he lifts
his haggard face, ravaged with self-doubts,
Peter sees he is not feeling well. Shadows
under his eye sockets 're shaped like full,
black moons. *You may ride
to the island on my Notebook,* he says, *if you wish,
only do not   misunderstand . . . Philosophy
is action.*

What W. calls his Notebook, Peter cannot see;
he can make out a kind of flat, wooden ferry . . .
that wasn't there — before Wittgenstein came.
*If I could think clearer, today, little rabbit,
I would explain it better.*
If I could come with you?
*Russell is on the island. I need to explain
in person, the new work, to him.*
*My words need me to interpret them or they
probably won't be understood.*

A dangerous delusion, grunts someone
whom Peter — up till now — has not seen —
who is squatting — rude & nameless —
on his haunches   further down
the chill, windless beach. *An author
cannot count on standing, like a fixture,
behind his or her work, propping*

*what he or she says
is its meaning up.
            Once words are printed
they are texts & anyone can talk to them
as they talk to & amongst themselves. One word
leans backward . . . taking meaning*

*from the words behind it . . . & forward . . . deferring
its meaning to what comes after it. In fact*

*life is one long, different kind of sentence;
the deferrals, there too, are endless, mate.
But as a concept, the author*

*as chief sauce-tipper   of the tomato sauce
of meaning, is, to put it crudely, somewhat smeared.*

Wittgenstein is starting to bang his hands
up & down on the air. He is either trying
to warm them, or he is getting cross. He *has*
been misunderstood.

Cancer, which has been listening too, beside Peter,
turns its head & walks quietly away. It has decided
to wait for Wittgenstein, somewhere up ahead.

Talk of deferral makes Peter's tummy rumble
like Mt Fuji would — if it were to start up.
He is not about to spit out
volcanic ash & baked rock, but his empty middle
is telling him something simple, about its state.
Perhaps, on the island, there will be food made

that a rabbit . . . might eat?
Mother-made onion soup? Or a sandy roof
with a string of brown onions hanging down
that a rabbit could stretch to & snitch?

They step onto the flat float of wood
so loaded with people, that, at the edges,
water is lapping over the planks. Peter
gets his paws wet & when he licks them
they taste not at all . . . like fur that has
been washed, in a sweet clean rain-drip shower,
in a tub on a burrow's sandy floor
in an age before nuclear waste.

After gliding over a windless expanse
that is smooth & polished
as a grey, silken stone,
after a while the ferry stops
& they clatter & patter off.
When Peter looks back —
at the grey
underwater —
he sees the ferry
has already
slipped down
like a red
autumn leaf
whose season
has gone.

The most corrupting of comforts is intellectual comfort.

Jacques Lacan

Paisaje con un Pájaro
or
Painting in a Wren?

Green whiskers curl across
the world outside
as if they were a screen.

Happy as a person who has left
a dark & reeking saucepan
behind, in a burntbean-flavoured kitchen,
I have climbed here to the almost-top:
it is as dark as the water soaking
in a saucepan
in which green beans
boiled, burnt & started to stink.

The voice of a male blue wren
light as the rubbing together
of the legs of a stick insect
chirrs in the greenblack foliage
of this tree.

A webmaker has trussed up
curls, coils, canoes of bark,
in a microcosm
of mosquito netting. Ants
climb at this level, twenty metres up:
it is their highway, right to the top,

& the blue wren
hops along their path
flicking his tail as if
he were on a private
trail, through the brush.
                        If you do not move
the ants will walk on you too
navigating agilely as if you were a part
of the ranges & valleys
of some mountain. They do not bite.
You are so still
blue wren takes you for tree
but sensing something awry
at the last
he gives his tail
a quick pleat
& scatters himself upward
into the blue air
that is too close
to be called stratosphere.
Parts of him are as blue as the butterflies
that drift down
through the tree's spaces, after him.
You were hoping
he would strut right up
& sidestep
flitting out on top of you.

a green evening

a million miles away from Lorca's
verde que te quiero verde

quietly moving their
grass coloured backs
as if a slight
wind were ruffling
the feathery lawn —

three metres from the
bmx track where a few
late
keen under-tens
go round —

two
red-rumped
grass parrot
couples
celebrate
the evening
with what the
day's sun
has brought them —
fresh
ripe
seeds of the soft, lime grass —

lifting   from time to time
young
green
juice-stained beaks

wonderingly
to look around

Looking for Some Tracks
(instead of making them)

The best poem you have ever written
hides like the Emmaville panther
dark/ myth/ uncomplicated by existence/
in a huge blackberry tangle
up the valley
beside the river.

You can hear it cough,
hear the dry snarl
as it moves its slight
animal's bulk, over sticks,
in the thicket's middle.

When your heart
stops pounding panic
& slows to an even
beat, you walk closer
& find the cat-tracks — entering or
                        leaving? —
larger
      than any you have ever seen.

You cannot tell, still,
with your nose stuck into spoor,
the tracks going into the thicket
from the tracks going out of it.

You've always been
a bad
reader of signs.
The surreal has been padding
to & fro
tearing up
the ground all night.

Your poem, like the panther,
fails to emerge.

Giving up
on the idea of hunting
a poem as if it were
an animal,
going home
through the ordinary scrub,
towards Emmaville,
your head
lost in abstraction,
you meet an
unimaginative, non-drunk,
bush-walking,
disbeliever-in-panthers

who describes to you
in hair-crisp detail, perfect
down to dimensions of paw-print,
the objective correlative
to your unseen panther.

It is now
his panther   quietly padding off
to kill some sheep
over in Deepwater.

Perhaps once   a pair of panthers
did fall, out of a travelling
circus truck (springing
out of their cage
that was smashed
by the accident)
& *escape   into the real bush*
round Deepwater or Emmaville?

You will be unable
to make your mind
move your feet
from the blackberry tangles
round the bad
simile of the panther
for at least
the next week.

Rear Vision

At Swansea under opaque sky
on oil-scented water of pearl-shell
a sextet of outsize people
are rod-fishing out of a boat.

Two of the fattest stand up and tip
like topheavy fruit in slow motion
out of the small boat-basket.
Which rocks. But remains upright.

Their muscled arms knifing through water
two fallen pear-bodies stroke for the shore
where grandmother waits toothless.
Her pale brown-blotched hands
flutter like bogong moths. She flaps
beside a rust-coloured ranch-wagon
which she has just moved
on to the bridge, to be closer
to the two in the dangerous water.

Looking forward in the rear vision mirror
you can see her behind you. You are helpless,
her mouth opening in a silent O.
Shark fins also
cut air, after prey, in these waters.

Though a mind's dread of shark
may fill a sea with blood,
the water stays pearl.
                      The next car
smashes her off the road.

An Impression of Minimalist Art in the Late Twentieth Century

A yellow
semi-deflated balloon
floats trapped
on a small
green circle
of water surrounded
by white
water lilies. Jagged
reeds fence the outer
water circle of it,
making palisade. Wind
would stretch
this balloon's rubber luck
thin as a condom
around nothing, pressing it up
against the submerged
pricks of the
flattened
fallen palm fronds.
It breaks with a soft
plosive,
sigh or an exhalation,
leaving no children.

The burst balloon's rubber
drifts slowly
down centuries of water
past the forms
of the swirling eels
and the sucking mouths
of their skinny offspring.
Going down without a self
through the centuries
it is seen as a yellow flower
or a floating petal
on a water lily garden
at Giverny. In the late
twentieth century,
it's ok, don't cry;
it is rubber!
Perfectly hygienic
to wear against the skin
to suck
or to throw away.
Ego leaves a mark on it
redundant as the whorls
of the first,
artist's finger prints.

As if

As if it has drunk
'not wisely but too well'
at all
the watering holes of the world,

a diminutive drinker
makes a rare
eastcoast appearance, arriving
in urban Sydney — as if

it were some jaded pop star
from the fleshpots of the Côte d'Azur
who'd been booked in
for a D grade Leagues Club circuit.
                              As it
drops down
onto the visitor's branch,

belied
by the perfect gait
of its
delicately moving
pink, miniature feet,

the control
of its deportment,

the diamond dove's
red eyes
give it a look

of one
with a perpetual hangover.

In areas
where permanent water's
harder to find
than a prohibition
state's whisky, the diamond dove
travels a lot, following
the wandering
god of the rain,
as a disciplined
nomad, accepting
that god's
pooled and laked leftovers
as benison.

Here, as it sips,
its whisky-drinker's eyes
stare back at it, in innocent
limpid, faithfully-misleading
reflection.

It is more at home
on a bar
of sand,
     going down
to drink, between
the pug-holes of dingoes.

Best Lies . . .

plead passionately
for all animals' 'rights to life'
while swatting to kill
flies that sit
on their squashed-pig & sauce
sandwiches

best lies log their only regrets
about the destruction
of trees in forests
in letters & poems
on paper made out of wood

best lies are 3-yr-old boys
throwing themselves as hero
into every rescue story they know

best lies
collect their dole or pension cheques
with *smiles*
without biting off the hands
of the post-person
for being 'late' by *forty-eight hours*

best lies
have to hit the street on schedule
have to appear
to be making a frail search
after 'truth'/best lies

have to convince yr palate
that they've come — in superlative season —
out of the best grapes their vines will grow

best lies deliver themselves
like secondhand babies
with minimum-fuss
via 'welfare' officers
to selected foster 'homes'

best lies know that somewhere
they are WANTED to be TRUE

best lies
go to the melbourne cup
on the lips of trainers
& under
the perfect muscles
of subtle phar lap look-alikes
that will lose

best lies
slip bland
as editors' kraft-cheese regrets
out of envelopes

best lies are always fit

best lies fit yr pocket
better than yr hand does

& pulling down
venetian blinds over both yr eyes
best lies will shade you
better than a coolibah — or —
if you're that way inclined —
waltz you off with the squatter's sheep

best lies
get their feet
scrabbled down
into hard earth
& ball up like echidnas
so that someone wanting to pick up
some Animal Truth
gets a handful of spines
instead of a rounded totality
in his grip

best lies gallop
over the wooden boards of people's
head-houses
like food-play-&-pee-filled
small wombats
aching to get their claws
into the game of someone's leg

best lies fail
to grow extra organs
on siamese-twins
or to restore to life
a lover who is dead

best lies go out in style
suave as french vowels
& come back wet/ drowned
reeking of brandy liqueurs

best lies grow into truth
when the occasion for them's dead

best lies congregate like disbelievers
round the geometric 'angles' of a proof

to prostrate themselves
towards mecca
might indicate 'belief'

best lies prostrate themselves
both in & out of mecca's hours
in any direction that contains
a tourist lamb ram ewe or wether
whose hand baas or bleats
with cash or credit cards

as sellers on their home ground
best lies are phototropic
bending like sunflowers
towards the Beams of the Chosen
Bearers of Bankcard

best lies
won't hold hands with each other
for fear that they'll feel false

best lies are as tough as bmx bikes
& go as fast downhill
they will crash into chookyards
& assassinate
whatsoever
cane-toady
statement you choose

best lie of all
is an unbelievable *truth*

her letter . . .

her letter came to them three days after she'd
suicided by jumping off a peak in the blue mountains

: what could i tell you?

that over
the near
dark escarpments
the mauve
distance
pours
into the valley
violet
light

into a cup?

that the yellow flowers rage
horsebelly tall in a mountain summer
late rain
has filled the gums' new tips
with fire?

that a hunting
kookaburra's look
at the ground
stabs as hard
& as sharp
as his beak?

that i was hungry for the country round taree
under a grey-white sky soft-feathered
with cloud
with rain in the air & in the birdsongs?

that the road to mudgee winds
over a low spine of mountain   out   onto the plain
    & when
you hit the plain the shade is gone
& the dappled tree-winds with it
that in high wind in timber the tree shadows
hurl themselves blank as old
wants for suicide at the road   that the child
    that stepped
from behind the bus   at portland
took only one step   to banish
the road   cut glass   & life-in-death?

that to move
down a road
as lines
take a page

one must
begin somewhere & what
went before

is unshown   as also
after

only the heat
hangs solid as a belonging
over the valley
in the sky's blue house

that presently
a person
who belongs
where she is going
will hang her life up as if it were a hat
above a ledge of air
& step out

Whistling the Fluff

When a dandelion's seed-head
is puffed off its stem,
by the shove
of a human's
blown breath
or a wind's
gusty exhalation,

the white fluff on
each seed

sails out
on top
as a wind-catcher;

the seed drops down
                        beneath
like a nude brown person
   descending
      by
       p
       a
       r
       a
       c
       h
       u
       t
       e
   the sky-well.

Naturally
when a seed
gets his/her feet wet
by landing in a
damp soak
or the black
ooze by a lakeshore,

the seed's feet
stick
and root
        rummaging round
in the lake
        for sustenance.

The stuck
transmogrified seed
if not
taken out
by some
gutblocked Duck of Chance
becomes part
of a whole new
green generation
of wind-, earth-, and
water-pushed,
waving
wild

gold-flowered
weed dandelions.

The fluff,
that insignificant
insubstantial stuff

that powered the flight
by catching wind
when its passenger couldn't,

becomes that part
of the dandelion's history

that's destroyed by weather.

worn money

everything   is for burning
even & particularly
those things which most
                              casually
you'd think to keep . . .

was the taker
nude when he
or she
numbfingeredly unhitched them
from the line
through the black
frost over Narrabundah?
did his or her
feet & hands
burn
with the cold?

David Brooks'
new jeans
fresh
from their first wash
drying out
on the iced
clothesline
in the black
frost over Narrabundah
travel out

on the hips of the unknown
swinging into morning:

fresh from the Mint
a fifty dollar note
passes out
into that great
mindless
adventure of
being: a stiff
crackling
thing of new currency

~

& who
will take them
from the taker?

~

jeans too
can pass
out of circulation
like worn money
slipping
into furnaces
on the
      withdrawing
hips of the dead

Riding Circles

The moon
filled
with shadowy contours
like a photo of a world, seen
from far off,
a round
white
     low moon
flat
on a grey
dusk-sky,

looks down
over the lights
of the April
Royal Show's
Ferris wheel;

from the top
of the Ferris,
swinging down
in a huge
round curve
through the stomach
swerving space,
the Ferris riders
circle toward

all the far
shrunk adults
being judged
for riding
calm
pill-deadened horses
in circles
on the ground below,

lights on the sideshow stalls
winking on
like landing lights
on runways
where tent-peggers' horses,
chihuahuasize, edgily wait,
to cross,
to enter
a bright
bangle of dirt, & 'glory'
will light a gallop.

Small above those riders
now at the apogee
of the Ferris,
the moon's moved up
on a ride of its ball: the earth.

subjective around lismore

beside a hill
growing a dense,
naturally-irregular

gumscrubhaircut,

the hill growing bananas

is like a head
with a short
back&sides; neckhigh lumps

which could be boils or carbuncles
— on a person —
ripen aggressive — under blue
plastic bags —
                aggro. packaged —
punchy — like, does anyone?,
the local toughs: viceblue
but different — if a blood-eye
was *all* yous got . . .
                      & truth: we didn't
get dropped down a mineshaft
out emmaville way, as rumour puts
some locals lost; there was
a reason, for that, which drinkers
will tell you, 4 or 5
times an hour, about —

                                        if you're not
local cops — though who
is growing marihuana & where
is something about which to nobody
anybody will talk — the population
of lismore
is composed
of 60,000 knees — some hairy, some balding —
that are used
to bending
to a warmer weather
as are also

the other parts some (4) to the going price
                    from brisbane for a contract-kill

we left our thug the ego-poem there
bashing up the local toughs

though outclassed by a deeper light
mafiablue coming through
from the other side of his glass

& just pissed off

fire flaring at night through fields of burning sugar
& anger red on black complete the lismore 'i'

Slugs Could Ski

Excluded by their otherness
from human
revulsion
compassion
or distress

if slugs could ski
they could do it

on the slime trails
from your
nostrils
to your lips.

This ground
is raw. It burns
where the
ski trails
cross it.

A handkerchief's
broad snow-plough
would drive
the agony in

sending in
an unfeeling
scraping Monster

like *NeverEnding Story*'s
rough-edged Rock Eater

to clean up the trace
of a small
messy skier.

That the agony
going
down your face
is part of your cold's
(slow-beginner)
skiing away
is of no consolation.

One look
at the Am-o-lin's
gross cream worms
squeezed out lined up
set hard with winter

that have to be
rubbed in —
to heal —
's enough
to set you screaming.

It takes Blue Jay
moving low

near the spindly end
of a saggy bough

                        curling
his song out

round the pinkwhite
                        dipping
tutuskirted blossoms

of the eucalyptus *leucoxylon rosea*
his territory — overhead —

to snatch your rage.

Unable to taste
the water from snow

or to sniff the crush
of a eucalypt leaf

mistrusting touch
rejecting hugs

reduced
to three senses —
seeing, hearing —
and pain —

of course you blame
your mother.

Your mouth open
ready to roar

your lungs gripped
in a wheezy bellow

your cracked lips
surprise themselves

opening on a pure
red cave

of silence.

Blue Jay above —
You hiccup towards him.

now if you could . . .

when the poem is finished
it is set hard
like a hot pour
of errant
Wollongong Crude
that's been, inadvertently,
trapped, flowed, slowed, cooled —
& impossibly surprised —
by itself — at itself — at finding
a roughcast pig-iron self —
in a part-cracked
one-off mould.
it is **too** set.
now if you could
you would
ruffle its surface up
poke a gum twig
where three or four
hot disturbed black
biting ants're
angrily rushing about
— there — for it to chew on —
into its mouth —
& plant a wad of pliant
drawl-enriched
minty-green chewie
somewhere about

that an imaginary hand
has just
removed, from an
imaginary mouth.

another 'red' lady

a red parrot's head
framed
in a brown
hollow of gumtree

the mate
stands sentinel
eyeing
the picture
adding
a little *ch ch*
anger/danger

as the two
two-legged walkers
get too close

the red head
withdraws
back into the hollow
leaving
the gum frame
innocent
of bird

Mother with Broom

(FROM SOME ARCHIVAL FOOTAGE
FOUND IN THE YEAR 2044 AD)

On bare (of tree or house)
bleached winter-white grass,
in some post-
Chernobyl-like landscape,
a young mad woman
with a post-natal belly
dances nude
in great slow circles
to an audience of one: a dead child :
whom she is carefully avoiding
touching with her eyes.
She is hopelessly miming
fuck with a broom
scraping its wood
hard
up and down
in her crotch. The child, who is not
the one the woman
has recently lost
from her belly,
is trailing her limbs pliant and lax
towards the earth
she will soon be a part of, over the edges of
the cart on which
unseen ones
have borne her to here. Wisps of fine

childlike hair
curl
around her face in a coronal. She has married death.
In her play clothes.
She is maybe six.
The mother
with a sweet
distant childlike smile
of a mind in a private place
continues her slow
bland yet
becoming more urgent
fuck with the broom. Does she
re-live
the dumb
moment of this child's
death's
conception? Or foretell the next?

Fifty years ago,
an invisible technical crew
set their equipment running
(hoping, perhaps, by chance
to catch some tell-tale
fragment of the unknown
human's
guttural or visceral utterance?
Catching, instead, themselves —)
The tips
of their boots and some legs
left unedited — in the left hand corner
— for the 'truth value', as are

their voices —
'Shoot her!' the cameramen scream.
She is authentic human
reaction to disaster.
They have
not come for her
but they
are happy to have found her.

Outside the time in which
she was filmed with the broom
yet temporal as the film
upon which she is caught
and with which
she is contemporaneous
the mother continues
implacably trying to fuck.

Woman as Jug/ Blue Lady Poem

A real thrillin' game
of the old fuckin' bull
I handed in today lady — the speaker
swaying on his way to get some
lifesustaining plonk
to put in the empty,
jug-like, blue
malleable container, it being
half after four — p.m. — he
having 'signed off'
from whatever it was
that he'd
       done — that he'd
dismissed — with such
mustard-mouthed self-derision.

Stout baby pigeons with stubs for tails
& shoulders built like sumo wrestlers
scatter, street-smart,
                  from the weaving,
mocking course
    his squash-a-bird-or-kick-it feet
might take — with viciousness —
over the Neild Avenue pavement. He

is heading roughly for the Cross & it's
too near for him to be sober-
sour — when he gets there. It was he
bashed in a glass

& timber door — late one
moon-away, bleakish night back in winter —
his need found a backstreet's junk — a
part white-ant-rotted spar of timber —
he used that — to spring his force through
into a renovated chicken shed where he
bashed you from your handbag, with its
food-money — thirty dollars.
(Another real unthrillin' game
of the old fuckin' bull,
that night, blue lady?)
Subliminal
glimpse, in a smash of glass,
he lives — like this? — & also
heaving bricks through car
back windows/ seizing/ by accident
of finder/ heroin stash in a worker's lunchbox/
cassettes — or better —
cash — to fill the thirsty mouth
of the mute & docile
greedy blue container.

All his seasons are in it:
whether it's empty or full.
Eyes say — he's not worth a song — ;
he makes his own: singing to no one
dancing to nothing.

When its mouth's full,
mouth to mouth, he & it
sway together, fucking deep,
having their own
bitter party . . .

He'd spit in your sheep-stupid face
if you offered help — food, a bed — money —
    & bash
you blind when your back
was turned — to steal
               some
of what you'd offered. There's too
much anger — & raging pride — for him to ever
get what the blue jug wants
except by raiding for it/ smash & grab/
against the world/ or perhaps —
if he could find one to gull — by conning
a holy innocent.

One day he'll thunk a person dead:
unless he does extra well by it,
he'll not remember killing anyone.
Not a crease on his paper face.
Not a scratch on the blue lady.

All his reasons live in the jug.
Empty or full is the only weather.
If it's full, it loves him.
It is
    his blue
           lady of the air
& true
      to him only.

Navigating Around Things

On the still
windless
Monday ground,
under the park gum,
clustered round its foot
& round the raised
roots of its toe-bones,

like a flock of creamy birds, crouched
heads down,
faking — eating grass seeds,

a motionless flock
of crunched cardboard cartons,
abandoned hollow
by the weekend's visiting humans. Galahs

navigate around this artefactual flock,
eyes only
on what is relevant to galahs. They

are stripping seeds, from the last
brown ears
of the summer's grasses.
                              Nearby
horses canter fast & crisp, cutting
the humans' cricket pitch
with their shod hooves,

as if they were clipping scones
from the rolled green dough
of its cosseted grasses.

They are making frost breaths
in the ovens of their bodies.

Steam huffs out
in whitish wisps, ahead of them.
Pungent hot-baked horse dung
snorts out at the other end.

Chunks of turf
're flung sideways
when they gallop, sodding an innocent

downwardly mobile, young professional
on an 'indefinite
unpaid vacation' — from a job

with a broking office; not at all
suspicious he's been

'floated', on the air current,
outside a high-up window,
like a Kleenex with snot on it, he's

wistfully taking pictures
of any kind of action,

from the kneeling posture — worshipfully close
to the lovely risk of the hooves —

with a pre-crash bought-in-Bali camera.

Eels glide, down in the emerald murk,
sidling up to the light, swaying
like live, delicate arms
severed from dreams
of Balinese child dancers.
They suck, & wave — & terrify
the ducks. The only music
a soft 'fuck' as their mouths
take a bread morsel downward.

In the season of the small ducks,
when these day-old downy venturers
first stagger
              onto the lilyleaf plates,
        & wo
           bb
             le
                off
              raw
                  live
into the astounding
              truths of the water,
the large eels suck like centripetal force
that drags the water
out of the bathtub
            & suddenly
in the dying dark
alone down an eel
goes a trustful fluffball.

Out on the lake, now — two
late-autumn duck parents,
calling mistrustfully.

                              Out
of a brood
of perhaps thirteen,
they've one
impulsive, casual,
jauntily-angstless survivor.

A small
sliver of moon
pale as a paperbark flower's
ghost spider
floats on the late-
blue, pre-dark sky — a moon
fraying at the edges
into wisps of white
like a child's worn-out
cotton undergarments
a moon
like a ghost child
of a grown moon
that is waiting
for its spirit's
next stage.
At the edge
of the moon, the sky
holds the
almost-rinsed-clear-of-colour
risk-dipped blue
tints of a bird's egg.

Incomplete Observation of Process

The brown rocking-chair
of the dove's tail
thrusts hard and regular
against the air
when dove
alights. (This rocking
is common to both sexes.)
As dove's feet grip
the steadying branch,
the rocking-chair loses momentum
becoming merely
a wedge of cinnamon feathers.
      There is something about
the way the chair rocks — at the beginning —
that reminds you
of mating. Thus when the chair slows —
and the rocking decreases —
it is like a sex drive
that runs out of 'puff' in mid
                    act/air/art,
becoming oxygenless,
gasping,
running backwards from
completion.
      When
a male dove courts, he pursues —
cuckcuckcuckoo —
              the female

to the edge
        of the branch, shoving —
with menace of a
                burly, disobeyed,
holstered traffic cop —
his portly body at her, till she
is pushed off
into space, takes flight,
retreats. A male
dove will pursue
the vanishing lady
with every line and centimetre of his body —
as a male painter might
the achieving of his masterwork:
my lady's *portrait?* — *cuckcuckcuckoo* —
she is his obsession.
Watching, you would think
female doves
shrinking, retreating, evading
had nothing
        in the genetic heritage
of each one's life 'plan'
but a 'plot'
for individual
genetic annihilation: *they* pursue
the single life with as much
                      apparent
edgy fervour
as the male doves pursue *them*.
Turtle-doves *seem to mate*
when the male wears the female's
evasions into exhaustion, rather than

as a coming together
out of mutual lust. He tramps her hard.
She gives herself
a bemused shake as if to make sure
she's still alive and everything's working,
then heads
straight out into the blue
disappearing so fast
that the male dove, left behind on the branch,
had he a brain like a human's,
might've imagined he dreamt her.

How the nest-syndrome
fits in with all this
it is a little difficult
to determine.

        A more
'open' vantage point
from which
        to 'draw'
some further
'telling observation'
might perhaps
        be that
of a sucking louse
on whichever
of the doves it is
does the nest construction:

. . . the sucking louse . . .
unbeknownst to itself . . .
always at risk . . .
when it's down
under the cover
of a feathery phrase
sucking lifeblood

a beaked head
reaches round
tweaks reprovingly
and squashes it.

the coffee

if your
meaning/food/meal has a
                        (simple)
shape like a snake's, then maybe
death's at one end
and dinner's at the other;
where you pick it up
determines what you get

also what kind of ... *snake*
some
can be eaten either end.

for reasons
of analogy dim light foggy trees
or the glasses too far up,
                        of the many
'things which are like'
kookaburras, some
are kookaburras, the rest are not.

                        (some
                        kookaburras WON'T

                        eat
                        snake ever)

the
analogy
rests
though it's in a thermos have some?
the coffee's not hot

They Do Well

Watching the pears'
soft life-bruised skins
vanish
inside red-whiskered bulbuls
you realise
what good bodies
the skins came from;
white sweet juice
is flung out
by the stabs
of each beak.
Great shuddery splashes of pear
darken the timber
deck beneath
as if
as they are eaten
the pearpeople are weeping
— spare my wife
   spare my child
   spare my husband
   spare me spare me —

Tears or blood.

Pearpeople's guts are gone
& the bulbuls show no mercy.

        A 'mechanic'
        at ripping out
        the gut
        of a bogong
        moth
        or a cicada
        is a bulbul.
        Bold. Restless. Quick.
                  They exist
outside the world of their Latin name
or the language's conceit.
Whether it is
a passive fruit
or a small
wind-shivered moth they take
                  & metamorphose
is a matter of indifference to them.
Pragmatic non-linguistic
survival mechanisms, they do well
in an urban wasteland
upon which sprout tufts
of hesitant trees.

Pycnonotus jocosus.
Introduced
resident of Sydney.
Black crested & scarlet bummed.
Acquisitive-eyed.
Beak like a pick.

At dusk
if you dim your ears
you will hear the dead moths turning
& the dead pears singing
as the bulbuls sing.

metamultiplexities

their
    names
        rattle
like stones
        in a
mind's
        pebble-holding
tin
   can:
      Barthes
            Derrida
                  Foucault
                        Lacan;

yet
   each
      one
gives a different sound
                to the hole
its stone occupies . . .

Emerson as Brahma

1

'If the red slayer think he slays
Or if the slain think he is slain,
They know not well the subtle ways
I keep, and pass, and turn again.'

That was Ralph Waldo Emerson
        — nineteenth century American —
speaking as Brahma.

~

That poem they wrote
was about

their dog that died
circling him

like an accident   like a hide
that was not

his own.

Ground, that was not his own.

~

The ground that was not his skin
circled the stiff body helplessly
till it became him.

∼

There is no connection
between part 1 of this poem — the words of
               Emerson-Brahma —

and their poem about their dog

who followed after.

∼

Though
out of the ground over a rotted head
which once ran   thoughts of Brahma

any dog alive
may dig a skull

any dog alive   earthmouthed   laughing —

∼

2

Yet
should the smoke
still be seen
curling upward — delicate blue — one hundred
years' fine Havanas — after — the Brahma
awareness
'll appear
fitwrap
for an afterdinner egoist
squatting out in the craphouse
to have smoked — Sublime — from.

Not that
he's smug about it — 'They reckon ill
who leave me out;
When me they fly, I am the wings;
I am the doubter and the doubt,
And I the hymn the Brahmin sings' —
        a terrible plainsing —
those priests —   chanting it —

~

The rest of another ground 's
nothing special — Mount
Kosciusko at dawn, day
                    seen by walkers returning
down
     to the snowline — in summer —
through the snowgums, over the snowline,
flakes like white cockatoos returning.

~

A snowflake 'like' a white cockatoo

      remains a snowflake
      till it melt
      subject
      to the changes
      of snowflakes.

~

Chorus & Protagonists

Over
Centennial Park —
where Patrick White
used to walk — above
where he wanted
               his ashes blent —
in the middle distance, black birds
flap & wrap themselves, as if
round invisible lumps of air. They look like
bits of coal-sheeny washing:
wind-caught undergarments from Greek tragedy.
Cah, they cry, they are both
chorus & protagonists, as they swoop & flap
their underclothes of death
low over the
small birds darting into the tea-tree thickets.

At dusk a different
conspicuous villain
sits in the huge fig, he is black
with a white-tipped tail, gold
rings round his eyes like a gypsy.
Casually swinging from the tip of his beak
like a silverblue sardine
he has stabbed from the blue
tin of the air, he holds, before taking up
to dismember, on the upper branch,
before the student-audience, his three

gawky ignorant fledglings,
one perfect
Dusky Wood Swallow.
The class is Dismemberment 1 (Life-Drama)
for about-to-graduate Currawongs.

for all . . . (1987)

for all
the human animal
's ability
to web its world
with the structures
of its thinking

no human really
knows why it dies

any more
than a beetle does

half a world away
under the Europe-winded sky

picking insects
on the ground of Scotland

some grouse have already
taken in
their deaths and die

swallowing insects swallowing fallout
from Chernobyl

pecking they have caught
their part of the death of the earth

swallowing
are swallowed up in it

innocent as the children of Poland
eating food drinking water
from their deathrich Polish earth

as the children of Australia
eat fruit jams from Poland

as the peoples from Europe
eat foods from the lands of Europe

and drink from the river supplies
Chernobyl fell into

as the produce of Europe
is loaded into scalebright schools
of container-fish ships

and insectwinged aeroplanes

to travel out half a world

away from the Europe-winded sky
to feed the peoples . . .

From HIV to Full-blown . . .

Moths blown away
from their deaths in the high country
die on the coast.

He will go, with his tears & his
typewriter, down below,
& type one more poem out
that he doesn't want to write.
His lover cannot hear it.
He is writing for those
of his friends still alive.

To them, he types, very slowly —
because his arms are shaking
& his skin
has the night-sweat fever:
All the faces you love
will become ash or dust
if only
you can wait long enough . . .

He has waited enough.

with the last of the light

twenty metres up
late-feeding white cockatoos
hang upside down
contorting themselves into banana shapes
to rip the orange palm-fruit
with their beaks

dog pee & duck piss
pull a dog's nose to the grass

the beak of a yellow-winged honeyeater
clicks sharply together as it
snaps again & again
on the trail of late insects

runners heave
asthmatically past
& toddlers' dreaming eyes beg ducks
to stay forever by blobs of bread
but the bread goes down too fast
it is all gone
& the ducks go with it

almost dark   a black swan claps
his wings' white undersides
on the water like thunder
the length of the lake

taking off for the night's
black flying

with the last of the light
a professional sleeper-out beds down
claiming for the night
by being there
the metre-thick nest
that is softer than a swan's
under the pines
in the resinous den of needles

he has hessian bags
to cover his head & his face
he may fly
over any earth he chooses

hovering loud as helicopters
mosquitoes
looking for bare flesh
bald skull a bloodfuelled ear
or vein-blue wrist
round his warm
sleeping form
whine but cannot reach him

Picking the Nits

Tied to a streetlamp post as in the past
    people hitched horses, and now
park dogs, two royal blue, three white
    and two liverwurst-coloured balloons
salute the Vietnam veterans,
    who walk, in 1987, some in patched bodies,
on semi-functional legs,
    to remember . . . the unreturning, and to prove —
as if adjusting Descartes —
    je marche, donc je suis, giving themselves to the day
as weather gives itself to the ground, without stint.
Beside the solid, lumpen Opera House, and the light,
    wind-lunged yachts on the harbour
that sail, from Bennelong Point as the wind breathes
    in, out, under the bridge, wherever sails are pushed,
today the vets walk by choice. They have been solicited.
    Crowds cheer, and people weep, as if
they are forgiving.
    Sun, which gives itself   utterly to the day,
without meaning anything by it, dries the veterans' skins
    without defoliating them. Time has blotted some
    of every body's atrocities
into dried ink, on written pages, in books of
    je t'accuse, je m'accuse.

    Behind eyes ride the paling colours
of flaming children, of murderous children.
    Behind eyes rides war, with all its defoliants
of the human heart, war with all its drugs

    of the rituals of action —
    the drugging, mechanical actions
of people on firing ranges, and at sideshows —
    toy rises, you shoot, hit toy falls, another rises,
you shoot — or bomb, or flame-throw. In wars
    all the live toys
shoot back: sometimes the target-shooter falls,
    sometimes the target. In wars you are ordered
    to put your blocking-piece,
between the forces you are with,
    that are hopefully, behind you, and the forces
you are opposing. Lose your life-toy, no one will pat you
    on the back, say bad luck soldier, you've lost
your toy, here's another. Exactly the same
    one-birth-one-death deal as you get in peace, except
in peace, it is not the same — you are not
    ordered to kill. Few die, in peace or in war,
on ground they have chosen. The selector
    of a battleground is seldom called upon
to kill on it, or to fertilize it
    with the blood and bones of his body.

Cochineal-pink
    and white azaleas, mounted against a
sandstone rockface, do not lose the petals of their skins
    like people peeled by chemicals. War lives
behind people's eyes like some surrealist film, and with
    the eyes of the blind, we salute
    where we think you stand, on ground that
hurts because it is so unforgiving. In the sixties
    I knew a countryboy from the Vic. wheatlands
who carried his army gun, as a boy his

    rabbit-shooting rifle, marked by a knife
with a notch for each
    known Vietnamese he'd scored. He was proud
of his tally. Whether the target came
    from the North or South, of the paddock,
age, or sex, of the rabbit, was not something
    he'd bothered overly much about at home;
at home or in 'Nam he'd done
    what he was told,
whether by dad or the sergeant.
    Had not shot, by mistake, Australians. If he is
alive now, he will be marching, belly-paunched, older,
    amazed   at his life as one of his rabbits would be —
if it were left alive, if   it could think.

The rest of their day goes by
    in the physical fashion of Sydney. As in the rest
of some brewer's dream of Australia,
    tin cans slant, tilted
up to mouths, and drunks slant angled
    ogling out at traffic.

Elsewhere,
out in the scrub, beetles sail like small brown
    furniture-polished *objets d'art*
from one side of the hiking track to the other.
    Some click, as the rifle bolt does, into its breech,
and some go zzzz.
    Heavy black power-shift and gear-change, overhead
in the hard black wing-shuffle of a bird's dark
    swerve, sideways from the scrub, to check what is:
people moving over ground so hard it sends

its pain upward, each further
step you limp sends bruised feet's message
　　　through your body. The centre of pain,
where the message
　　　comes from, is the brain. However feeble.

Dog with brown saliva-and-dirt-sodden ball
　　　that it is carrying in its mouth so the two
humans with it won't forget
　　　its most precious
joy-tool. A toy, which is not
　　　its life, but which
puts a polish of joy on shared living. Honeysuckle's
　　　little penises — cream and corn-yellow
on the same tendril — drench the air
　　　with their sweet potent song. This
honeysuckle's leaves are the playgrounds
　　　of small insects; the leaves' elongated ovals
are the green of a watered lawn on sandy soil.
Picked, these leaves
　　　curl and turn inwards, as they die. They die twisting
and twisted.
　　　Some people pick honeysuckle and put it
between the pages of a book, to remind
themselves of something. Lost between the pages
　　　of a book, when they find it, they've forgotten
what such honeysuckle meant. In your mind
　　　as on a picked and dying tendril, the scent
of honeysuckle lingers.

~

It has been fashionable for America to see itself
    as the literate Ape
conscientiously picking the nits
    of its acts in Vietnam
from the fur of its belly, to examine them
    and crack them, censuring itself with its teeth.
Now, it is into acceptance. Perhaps Australia too
    is past its nit-picking . . . into acceptance.

The Vietnam War too has been picked.
    It is the past.
It smells of horror terror flesh on fire.
Water on ash, flame gone out, steam rising.
The scent of faded flesh on fire
sticks, peeling and clinging, to the flesh of memory.

The National Glue — What Goes Down . . . Must Come Up?

If the nation's
glue
is too strong,
and you lick a lot, it will
make you sick. (Work
for Australia Post, you
will find this out.)

Or work, in your head, with your
imagination, working out
the how

of the rise of
German nationalism, concurrent
with the rise of
Adolf Hitler, and the Nazis: this too
induces nausea,
the manifestation of which
a doctor calls: vomit, a physical
law of the gut.

Or, have in your hands, the protest letters
of a class of primary school children,
which they want
lick-sealed
and sunk
in a letter-box . . .

~

Seven sheets of A4 paper
are strong enough
to break the leg of a pin.

~

In the context
of a contest between forces,

it is the strength of the paper
which snaps the pin;

the strength of the writing
on
the paper
       is irrelevant.

~

Though it varnishes your tongue
to perfection,
the glue on the new stamps
is too weak
to hold the perforated,
butterfly-wing thin, white
paper edges down.

~

Whether it is
two centuries'
accumulated guilt,
over a buried
theft,
of Australia, accompanied by
unacknowledged, unpunished murders,
or too much swallowed glue,
what goes down, must come up.
La Rochefoucauld's
law — of the vomiting psyche.

~

The 'artwork' on the stamps,
two,
crudely drawn,
blue and pink,
'thick' Australian children,
complacently turning
their fat faces
towards the 'celebration'
of Australia's 1988 'birthday',
embraces theft warmly,
by calling it something else.

The stamp design denies
white id its right to vomit,
black psyche its right to rage.

Or even to acknowledge, haul up, look at
what was done.

~

On the stamp, two
heavy, blond, Aryan-looking children
anticipate greedily munching
gross wedges of bicentennial cake

as many of the real,
pink, yellow, brown,
olive, white, dark-
skinned children from the many
cultures in this primary school,

do not . . . hot-faced with modern shame
        at ancient bloody acts
        (familiar to them
        as instant coffee or
        hot water out of a tap).
        Their recurrent views . . . express simply . . .
        if it'd been me, alive then,
        I wouldn't have . . .
        stolen their land . . . but (a consensus)
        if a spear came at you,
        you would have to send one back . . .

~

The stamps
on the children's protest letters

lift off

and curl up at the edges,
playing an active
game to subvert
gravity, all the way
to the large
red prick
that belongs to Australia Post,
where gravity
wins —
false children's faces on curled-up stamps,
and envelopes,
go sailing — briefly twinned and flat —
down to bed in the
all-people's, unhistoric,
childish, contemporary dark.

NOTES

1 **Doily** *sb.* or *a.* Also **doiley, doyly, -ley,** *erron.* **d'Oyley, d'oylie**. [from personal surname *Doiley* or *Doyley*.

1712 BUDGELL *Spect.* No. 283 para. 18 The famous Doily is still fresh in every one's Memory, who raised a Fortune by finding out Materials for such Stuffs as might at once be cheap and genteel. **1727** SIR H. SLOANE in *Phil. Trans.* XXXIV. 222 Mr. Doyly, (who was a great searcher after Curiosities, and gave his Name to a sort of Stuffs worn in Summer). **1750–1800** PEGGE *M.S. Note* (Skeat, *Philol. Trans.* 1885, 91) Doyley kept a Linnen-draper's shop in the Strand, a little West of Catherine Street.]

†1. *attrib.* or *adj.* The name of a woollen stuff, 'at once cheap and genteel', introduced for summer wear in the latter part of the 17th c. Obs.

1678 DRYDEN *Kind Keeper* IV. i Some Doily Petticoats, and Manto's we have. **1697** *Lond. Gazette* No. 3293/4 A sad colour Doyly Drugget new Coat. **1712** ARBUTHNOT *John Bull* 1.vi His children were reduced from rich silks to Doily stuffs. **1713** ADDISON *Guardian* No. 100 para. 2 Summer has often caught me in my Drap de Berry, and winter in my Doily suit. **1714** GAY *Trivia* 1. 43 Now in thy trunk the D'oily habit fold, The silken drugget ill can fence the cold.

2. *sb.* (Originally Doily-napkin.) A small ornamental napkin used at dessert.

1711 SWIFT *Jrnl. to Stella* 23 Apr., After dinner we had coarse Doiley-napkins, fringed at each end, upon the table to drink with. **1785–95** WOLCOTT (P. Pindar) *Lousiad* 11. Wks. 1. 243 Who dares with Doylies des'perate war to wage. **1798** *Gentl. Mag.* LXVIII. 11. 755/2 Thus also the small table napkin called a *D'Oyley*. **1802** S. ROGERS in Clayden *Early Life* (1887) 437 After dinner (in Paris) she threw about her some ugly and dirty English doyleys, which she also explained as the English fashion, and of which I felt quite ashamed. **1855** H. MARTINEAU *Autobiog.* (1877) I. 68 I had been picking at the fringe of my doily.

2 **Cucumber frame** Horticultural device, of glass and wood, used in cold climates to protect frost-tender cucumber seedlings from death, and to speed growth, the glass acting as a sun-trap.

1944 ANON. *P. H. Lepus: Early Life* p.118 In the earlier part of the twentieth century on journeys to some of the Great Vegetable Gardens of Britain, Peter Lepus learnt to associate cucumber frames with the presence of edibles. **1994** LEPUS, P. H. *Travels Vol. 1* p.22 I have always found cucumbers where there were cucumber frames.